ANGLESEY INFANT SCHOOL

ABCDEFGHIJKLMNOPQRS
abcdefg hijklmn opqrs tuvwxyz

Contents

1	Words about Animals	2
2	Words Around You —	
	Buildings and Places	19
	The Home	31
3	Words about People	38
	The Body	50
	Clothes	51
	Food and Drink	53
4	Words about Plants	64
5	Words about Transport	71
6	Other Words — All Sorts	78
	Where	93
	Action Words	94
	Colours	98
	Numbers	99
	Time	100
7	Index	102

Words about Animals

Aa

alligator — An **alligator** is a large reptile that lives in rivers and swamps in America and China.

Alsatian — An **Alsatian** is a large dog often used by the police.

amphibian — An **amphibian** lives both on land and in water.

animal — An **animal** is any living thing that is not a plant.

ant — An **ant** is a tiny insect. Ants live together and are very busy.

antelope — An **antelope** looks like a deer.

Bb

badger — A **badger** is a wild animal about the size of a small dog.

bat — A **bat** looks like a mouse with wings.

bear — A **bear** is a very big, heavy, wild animal.

beaver — A **beaver** lives in water as well as on land.

Animals

bee	A **bee** makes honey and lives in a hive.
beetle	A **beetle** is an insect with hard skin like a shell.
bird	A **bird** has feathers, two wings, two legs and lays eggs.
blackbird	A **blackbird** is a song-bird.
blue tit	A **blue tit** is a tiny bird often seen in gardens.
budgerigar	A **budgerigar** looks like a small parrot and is often kept as a pet.
buffalo	A **buffalo** is a large, wild North American animal.
bull	A **bull** is a male farm animal.
bulldog	A **bulldog** is a strong, brave dog.
butterfly	A **butterfly** is an insect with four, large coloured wings.

Cc

calf	A **calf** is a young cow or young bull.
camel	A **camel** lives in the desert.

Animals

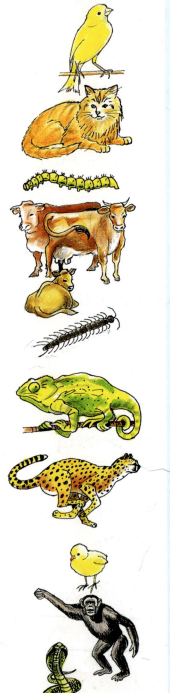

canary — A **canary** is a small song-bird often kept as a pet.

cat — A **cat** is a small, furry animal usually kept as a pet.

caterpillar — A **caterpillar** is a grub that turns into a butterfly or moth.

cattle — **Cattle** are farm animals such as cows, bulls and calves.

centipede — A **centipede** is a crawling insect with many pairs of legs.

chameleon — A **chameleon** is a small lizard that can change its colour.

cheetah — A **cheetah** is a large wild cat which can run very fast.

chicken — A **chicken** is a young hen or cock.

chimpanzee — A **chimpanzee** is a kind of ape.

cobra — A **cobra** is a poisonous snake.

cow — A **cow** is a large farm animal which gives us milk.

crab — A **crab** has a hard shell and strong claws. It lives in the sea.

Animals

crocodile — A **crocodile** is a large and dangerous reptile that lives in rivers and lakes in some hot lands.

crow — A **crow** is a large, black bird.

cub — A **cub** is a young fox, bear, wolf, lion or tiger.

Dd

dachshund — A **dachshund** is a small dog with a long body and very short legs.

daddy longlegs — A **daddy longlegs** is a flying insect.

Dalmatian — A **Dalmatian** is a large white dog with black spots.

deer — The **deer** is a fast animal that eats grass. Some deer have antlers.

dinosaur — The **dinosaur** was a very large reptile that lived millions of years ago.

dog — The **dog** is a favourite pet. Some work on farms and others are guard dogs.

dolphin — The **dolphin** lives in the sea. It looks like a small whale and is very intelligent.

Animals

donkey	A **donkey** looks like a small horse.
dove	The **dove** is a kind of pigeon.
dragonfly	The **dragonfly** is a large insect with long legs and four wings.
duck	The **duck** is a bird. It can swim and quack.

Ee

eagle	An **eagle** is a large bird. It carries off small animals.
earwig	An **earwig** is a small insect often found on flowers.
eel	An **eel** is a long, thin fish which looks like a snake.
elephant	The **elephant** is the largest land animal. It lives in Africa and India.
emu	An **emu** is a large Australian bird which cannot fly.

Ff

fawn	A **fawn** is a young deer.
fish	A **fish** lives and breathes in water.
flamingo	A **flamingo** is a bird with long legs and pink feathers.

Animals

fly — A **fly** is an insect with two wings.

foal — A **foal** is a baby horse.

fox — A **fox** looks like a dog with a long, bushy tail.

frog — A **frog** is a small jumping animal. It can live on land or in water.

Gg

gerbil — A **gerbil** is a small, furry animal. It can be kept as a pet in a cage.

giraffe — A **giraffe** is a tall animal with a very long neck and long legs. It comes from Africa.

goat — A **goat** is an animal kept for its milk, meat and wool.

goldfish — A **goldfish** is a small orange-red fish kept as a pet.

goose — A **goose** is a bird that looks like a large duck.

gorilla — The **gorilla** is the largest and strongest kind of ape.

grasshopper — A **grasshopper** is a small insect that uses its long back legs to jump.

Animals

greyhound — A **greyhound** is a dog. It is a very fast runner.

guinea pig — A **guinea pig** is a small, furry animal without a tail often kept as a pet.

Hh

hamster — A **hamster** is a small animal that looks like a large mouse. It keeps food in its cheeks.

hare — A **hare** is a wild animal, larger than a rabbit.

hawk — The **hawk** is a bird with a sharp beak and curved claws.

hedgehog — A **hedgehog** is a small animal with prickles on its back.

hen — A **hen** lays eggs.

heron — A **heron** is a large bird which eats fish.

herring — A **herring** is a small sea fish that is caught for food.

hippopotamus — A **hippopotamus** is a very large animal which lives in the rivers of Africa.

Animals

horse — A **horse** is a farm animal used for riding and pulling coaches and carts.

husky — A **husky** is a strong dog, used in very cold lands to pull sledges.

Ii

insect — An **insect** has six legs.

Jj

jaguar — A **jaguar** looks like a leopard. It lives in South America.

Kk

kangaroo — The **kangaroo** lives in Australia and jumps on its back legs. It carries its young in a pouch.

kingfisher — A **kingfisher** lives near water and dives for fish.

kitten — A **kitten** is a young cat.

kiwi — A **kiwi** is a New Zealand bird that cannot fly.

koala — A **koala** is a timid Australian animal which lives in eucalyptus trees.

Ll

Labrador — A **Labrador** is a large dog often used as a guide dog for blind people.

ladybird — A **ladybird** is a small spotted beetle that flies.

Animals

lamb — A **lamb** is a young sheep.

leopard — A **leopard** is a large wild cat from Africa and Asia. It has spots.

lion — A **lion** is a very large, strong cat found in Africa and Asia.

lizard — A **lizard** is a reptile with four short legs and a long tail.

lobster — A **lobster** lives in the sea and is good to eat.

Mm

mackerel — A **mackerel** is a sea fish which is caught and eaten.

magpie — A **magpie** is a noisy, black and white bird.

mammal — A **mammal** is an animal that gives milk to its young.

mammoth — A **mammoth** was a kind of hairy elephant which lived very many years ago.

mole — A **mole** is small and furry. It tunnels underground and makes molehills.

monkey — A **monkey** is a long-tailed animal. It spends a lot of time in trees.

Animals

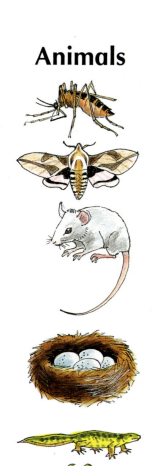

mosquito — A **mosquito** is a small insect which bites.

moth — A **moth** is an insect that looks like a butterfly. It usually flies at night.

mouse — The **mouse** is small with sharp teeth and a long tail.

Nn

nest — A **nest** is a home an animal makes for its young.

newt — A **newt** is a small animal. It lives in water and on land.

Oo

octopus — An **octopus** lives in the sea. It has eight arms.

orangutan — An **orangutan** is a large ape from Asia.

osprey — An **osprey** is a large bird that feeds on fish.

ostrich — The **ostrich** is the largest bird in the world but cannot fly. It has a long neck and long legs.

otter — An **otter** lives in or near water. It is a good swimmer and feeds on fish.

Animals

owl	An **owl** is a bird with a big head and big eyes. It hunts for food at night.
ox	An **ox** is like a cow. It is used to pull carts.
oyster	An **oyster** is a small, flat shellfish which is eaten.

Pp

panda	A **panda** is black-and-white and looks like a small bear. It comes from China.

panther	A **panther** is a kind of leopard.

parrot	A **parrot** is a bird with brightly coloured feathers. It can be taught to talk.

peacock	A **peacock** is a large male bird with a large tail that opens like a fan. The female is called a peahen.

pelican	A **pelican** is a large sea bird. It has a pouch under its beak where it stores the fish it catches.

penguin	A **penguin** is a sea bird that swims but cannot fly.

Animals

perch — A **perch** is a small fish that lives in rivers and lakes.

pheasant — A **pheasant** is a large bird. The cock pheasant has a long, colourful tail.

pig — The **pig** is a farm animal kept for its meat called pork, bacon or ham.

pigeon — The **pigeon** is a large bird. It can fly a long way and find its way home.

pike — A **pike** is a big freshwater fish with very sharp teeth.

plaice — A **plaice** is a flat sea fish which is eaten for food.

polar bear — The **polar bear** is a large animal which lives in the cold lands of the north.

pony — A **pony** is a small horse.

prawn — A **prawn** is a shellfish like a large shrimp.

puffin — A **puffin** is a sea bird. It has a short thick beak.

puppy — A **puppy** is a young dog.

Animals

	python	A **python** is a large snake.

Rr

	rabbit	The **rabbit** has soft fur and long ears. Some rabbits are kept in hutches.
	rat	The **rat** looks like a large mouse. It has sharp teeth and a long tail.
	rattlesnake	A **rattlesnake** is poisonous. Its tail makes a rattling noise.
	reindeer	The **reindeer** is a large deer with antlers which lives in the cold lands.
	reptile	A **reptile** has cold blood. Its body is covered with scales.
	rhinoceros	The **rhinoceros** is a large, fierce animal found in Africa and India.
	robin	The **robin** is a small bird. The robin has a red breast.
	rook	The **rook** is a large, black bird. They nest together in rookeries.

Ss

	salmon	The **salmon** is a large fish with pink flesh.
	sardine	The **sardine** is a small, silvery fish.

Animals

	scorpion	The **scorpion** is an insect with a long tail and a poisonous sting.
	seagull	The **seagull** is a large bird which lives near the sea. It makes a loud, screeching noise.
	seahorse	The **seahorse** is a very small fish which has a head like a horse.
	seal	The **seal** is a large, furry sea animal.
	shark	The **shark** is a very large sea fish which has many sharp teeth.
	sheep	The **sheep** is a farm animal kept for its wool and meat.
	shrimp	A **shrimp** is a small grey shellfish which turns pink when it is cooked.
	slug	The **slug** looks like a snail without a shell.
	snail	The **snail** is a small animal with a shell. It moves slowly and leaves a silver trail.
	snake	The **snake** is a long and thin reptile without legs.

Animals

sparrow — The **sparrow** is a small brown and grey bird found in towns.

spider — The **spider** is a very small creature with eight legs and no wings. It catches insects in its web.

squirrel — A **squirrel** is a small grey or red animal with a bushy tail.

starfish — A **starfish** is a small sea creature.

starling — The **starling** is a bird with dark, shiny feathers.

stickleback — The **stickleback** is a tiny fish which lives in ponds and rivers. It has spines on its back.

stoat — The **stoat** is a small fierce wild animal which eats smaller animals.

stork — The **stork** is a large bird. It sometimes nests on house chimneys.

swallow — The **swallow** is a bird. They fly away to warm countries for the winter.

swan — The **swan** is a beautiful white bird which lives on rivers and lakes.

Tt

tadpole — The **tadpole** is a young frog or toad.

Animals

termite — A **termite** is an insect that looks like an ant. It eats wood.

terrier — A **terrier** is a small, short-haired dog.

thrush — The **thrush** is a brown bird with a spotted breast. It sings sweetly.

tiger — The **tiger** is a large fierce animal. It is a member of the cat family.

toad — A **toad** is a frog-like animal with a rough lumpy skin.

tortoise — The **tortoise** is kept as a pet. It moves slowly and can pull its head and legs into its shell.

trout — A **trout** is a fresh water fish. It is good to eat.

turkey — A **turkey** is a large bird which can be eaten.

turtle — The **turtle** has a shell like a tortoise. It lives in the sea and on land.

Vv

vulture — The **vulture** is a very large bird which feeds on dead animals.

Animals

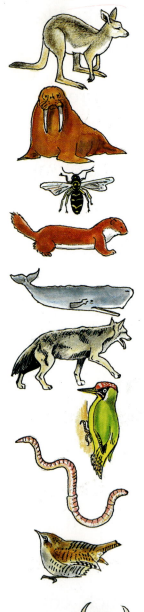

Ww

wallaby — The **wallaby** is a small kind of kangaroo.

walrus — The **walrus** is a large sea animal with tusks.

wasp — A **wasp** is a flying insect which can sting.

weasel — The **weasel** is a wild, fierce animal. It lives on birds and mice.

whale — The **whale** is the largest of all animals. It lives in the sea.

wolf — The **wolf** is a wild animal which looks like a large dog.

woodpecker — The **woodpecker** is a bird. It pecks holes in trees with its beak to get insects.

worm — The **worm** has a soft, thin body and no legs. It lives in the soil.

wren — The **wren** is a very small song-bird.

Yy

yak — The **yak** is a long-haired ox from Asia.

Zz

zebra — The **zebra** is a wild animal from Africa. It looks like a horse with stripes.

Words Around You — Buildings and Places

Aa

abbey — Monks or nuns live and work in an **abbey**.

airport — Aeroplanes fly from an **airport**.

apartment — An **apartment** is a group of rooms to live in.

aviary — Birds are kept in an **aviary**.

Bb

bakery — A baker bakes bread and cakes in a **bakery**.

barn — A farmer stores grain, hay and other crops in a **barn**.

bay — A **bay** is a curved part of the seashore.

beach — The **beach** is the sand or pebbles at the seaside.

boutique — A **boutique** is a small shop selling modern things such as clothes.

bridge — A **bridge** is built over a road or water or railway line so that people and vehicles can cross.

bungalow — A **bungalow** is a house with all its rooms on the ground floor.

2

Buildings and Places

	bus station	Buses start their journey at a **bus station**.

Cc

	cabin	A **cabin** is a room on a boat for passengers.
	café	Meals and snacks are served in a **café**.
	cage	Animals or birds are sometimes kept in a **cage**.
	camp	A **camp** is where tents are set up.
	canal	A **canal** is made for boats and barges to sail on.
	car park	People leave their cars in a **car park** while they go shopping.
	castle	A **castle** is an old building with high walls to protect those inside.
	cathedral	A **cathedral** is a very large church in a city.
	cave	A **cave** is a big hole in the ground or in the side of a rock.
	cell	A **cell** is a small room in a prison.
	cellar	A **cellar** is a room under the house.

Buildings and Places

chapel	A **chapel** is a small church.
church	People go to **church** to pray.
cinema	Films are shown in a **cinema**.
circus	A **circus** is a travelling show with animals, clowns and acrobats.
city	A **city** is a large town.
classroom	A **classroom** is a room in a school.
cliff	A **cliff** is high, steep land often at the edge of the sea.
clinic	Doctors and nurses give help to people in a **clinic**.
coast	The **coast** is where the sea and land meet.

Dd

desert	A **desert** is usually hot and sandy or stony. Very few plants grow in the desert.
dock	Ships are loaded and unloaded at a **dock**.

Ff

factory	People make things in a **factory**.

Buildings and Places

fair — A **fair** is a place for fun with roundabouts and sideshows.

farm — A **farm** is where food is grown and animals are kept.

field — A **field** is part of the farm where crops are grown and animals feed.

fire station — The **fire station** is the place where fire engines are kept.

flats — **Flats** are a number of homes, usually in a high building. A **flat** has a number of rooms where people live.

forest — A **forest** has lots of trees.

Gg

garage — Petrol and oil are sold at a **garage**. Cars are serviced and repaired there.

garden — Land where flowers, grass and vegetables are grown is called a **garden**.

greenhouse — A **greenhouse** is made of glass to keep plants warm.

gymnasium — A **gymnasium** is a large room where people can keep fit and play sports.

Buildings and Places

Hh

hall — A **hall** is a very big room where meetings and concerts are held.

hangar — Aeroplanes are kept in a **hangar**.

harbour — A **harbour** is a place for ships and boats to stay.

hill — A **hill** is a raised piece of land, lower than a mountain.

hospital — A **hospital** is where sick people are cared for by doctors and nurses.

hotel — People pay to eat and sleep in a **hotel**.

house — A **house** is where people live.

hut — A **hut** is a small wooden building like a shed.

hutch — Pet rabbits or guinea pigs are kept in a **hutch**.

Ii

igloo — An **igloo** is an eskimo hut made of blocks of hard snow.

inn — An **inn** is like a small hotel where people can buy drinks and food.

23

Buildings and Places

island	An **island** is a piece of land with water all round it.

Jj

junction	A **junction** is where two or more roads or railway lines meet.

jungle	The **jungle** is very hot and damp with lots of trees, plants and animals.

Kk

kennel	A **kennel** is a small hut for a dog to sleep in.

Ll

laboratory	Scientists work in a **laboratory**.

lake	A **lake** is a large stretch of water with land all around.

lane	A **lane** is a narrow road in the country.

launching pad	Rockets, space-shuttles and space ships are fired into the air from a **launching pad**.

launderette	People go to a **launderette** to wash and dry clothes.

lawn	A **lawn** is grass kept cut and tidy, usually by a house.

Buildings and Places

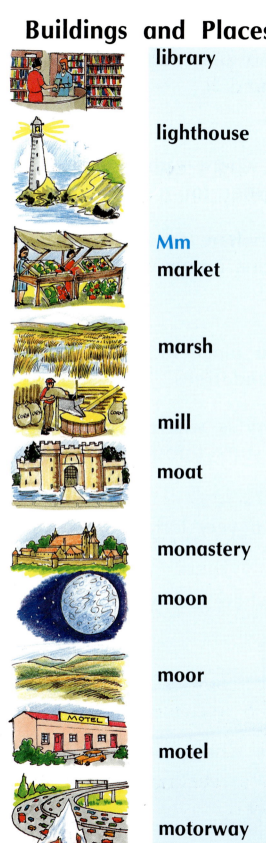

library	A room or building full of books is called a **library**.
lighthouse	A **lighthouse** is a tower with a flashing light to warn ships about rocks.

Mm

market	There are usually stalls in a **market** where people buy and sell things.
marsh	A **marsh** is a piece of soft, wet ground.
mill	Corn is ground into flour at a **mill**.
moat	A **moat** is a ditch, filled with water, around a castle.
monastery	Monks live and work in a **monastery**.
moon	The **moon** is the large, bright object that shines in the sky at night.
moor	A **moor** is hilly, rough ground where grass and heather grow.
motel	A **motel** is a hotel used by people with cars.
motorway	A **motorway** is a wide, fast road.
mountain	A **mountain** is a high hill.

25

Buildings and Places

museum — Old and interesting things are kept in a **museum**.

Nn

nursery (1) — A **nursery** is where small children are looked after for a short time.

nursery (2) — A **nursery** is where flowers, trees and plants are grown.

Oo

oasis — An **oasis** is a place in the desert with water and trees.

observatory — An **observatory** is where scientists look at the stars through a huge telescope.

ocean — An **ocean** is a very large stretch of sea water.

office — An **office** is where clerks and typists work.

oilrig — An **oilrig** is used to get oil from under the sea.

orchard — An **orchard** is where many fruit trees grow.

outback — The **outback** is the country parts of Australia that are far from cities and towns.

Buildings and Places

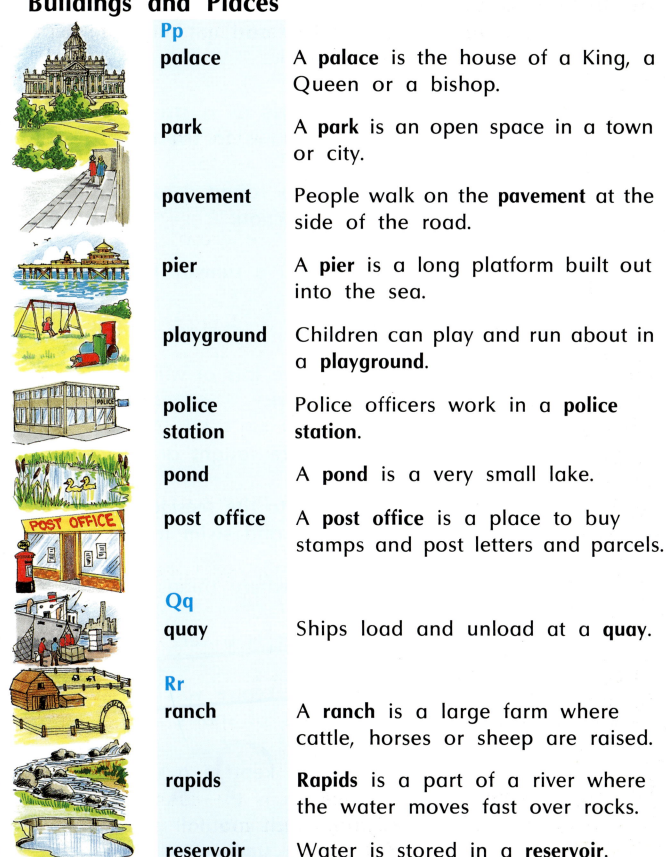

Pp

palace	A **palace** is the house of a King, a Queen or a bishop.
park	A **park** is an open space in a town or city.
pavement	People walk on the **pavement** at the side of the road.
pier	A **pier** is a long platform built out into the sea.
playground	Children can play and run about in a **playground**.
police station	Police officers work in a **police station**.
pond	A **pond** is a very small lake.
post office	A **post office** is a place to buy stamps and post letters and parcels.

Qq

quay	Ships load and unload at a **quay**.

Rr

ranch	A **ranch** is a large farm where cattle, horses or sheep are raised.
rapids	**Rapids** is a part of a river where the water moves fast over rocks.
reservoir	Water is stored in a **reservoir**.

Buildings and Places

restaurant — People buy and eat meals in a **restaurant**.

river — A **river** starts as a stream in the hills and flows to the sea.

roundabout — Traffic goes round a **roundabout** at a busy junction.

runway — Aircraft use a **runway** to land and take off.

Ss

safari park — You can see lots of wild animals in a **safari park**.

school — Children are taught at **school**.

seaside — People go to the **seaside** to play on the beach and swim in the sea.

shop — A **shop** is where things are sold.

skyscraper — A **skyscraper** is a very tall building.

sports centre — At a **sports centre** you can play many kinds of sports.

stable — Horses are kept in a **stable**.

stadium — People watch football and other sports at a **stadium**.

Buildings and Places

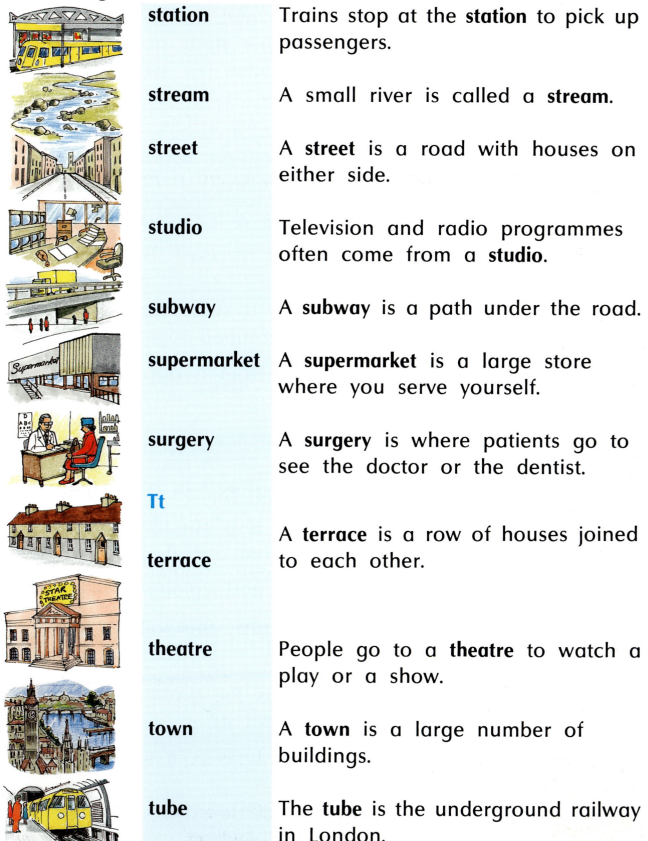

station	Trains stop at the **station** to pick up passengers.
stream	A small river is called a **stream**.
street	A **street** is a road with houses on either side.
studio	Television and radio programmes often come from a **studio**.
subway	A **subway** is a path under the road.
supermarket	A **supermarket** is a large store where you serve yourself.
surgery	A **surgery** is where patients go to see the doctor or the dentist.

Tt

terrace	A **terrace** is a row of houses joined to each other.
theatre	People go to a **theatre** to watch a play or a show.
town	A **town** is a large number of buildings.
tube	The **tube** is the underground railway in London.

Buildings and Places

Uu

university — Clever people study at **university** after they have left school.

Vv

valley — The land between two mountains or hills is a **valley**.

viaduct — A **viaduct** is a long bridge which carries a road or railway over a valley.

village — A **village** is a small number of buildings grouped together.

volcano — Lava flows from a **volcano** when it erupts.

Ww

warehouse — Goods are stored in a **warehouse**.

waterfall — A **waterfall** is a stream of water tumbling from a high place.

wharf — Ships load and unload at a **wharf.**

windmill — The wind turns the sails of a **windmill**.

world — The **world** is the earth and everything on it.

Zz

zoo — Wild and rare animals are kept in a **zoo**.

The Home

Aa

aerial — An **aerial** helps to bring pictures and sounds to your television or radio.

armchair — An **armchair** is a soft and comfortable chair.

Bb

bath — The **bath** is used to wash the body.

bathroom — A toilet, washbasin, bath and shower are often in a **bathroom**.

bed — At night we sleep in a **bed**.

blanket — A **blanket** keeps us warm in bed.

bookcase — Books are kept on shelves in a **bookcase**.

bricks — Walls are made of **bricks**.

brush — A **brush** is used to sweep the floor.

bucket — A **bucket** is used for carrying water.

Cc

carpet — A **carpet** is a thick, soft covering for the floor.

ceiling — The **ceiling** is the inside roof of a room.

chair — A **chair** is a seat with a back.

31

The Home

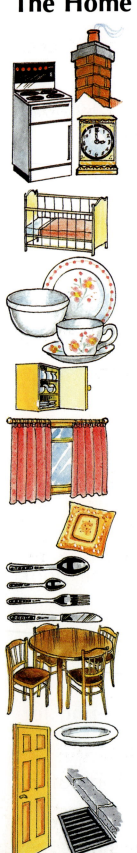

chimney	Smoke from a fire goes up through the **chimney**.
clock	The time is shown on a **clock**.
cooker	A **cooker** is used to cook food.
cot	A baby's bed is called a **cot**.
crockery	Cups, saucers, plates and basins are **crockery**.
cup	We drink from a **cup**.
cupboard	Things are stored in a **cupboard.**
curtains	**Curtains** are made of cloth. They hang at windows.
cushion	A **cushion** is soft to sit on.
cutlery	Knives, forks and spoons are **cutlery**.

Dd

dining-room	Meals are eaten in the **dining-room**.
dish	A **dish** is like a plate with a rim.
door	A **door** is a way in or out of a house or room.
drain	Dirty water and waste go down the **drain**.

The Home

drawer	A **drawer** is a sliding box in a piece of furniture.
dressing table	A **dressing table** is in the bedroom. It has drawers and a mirror.
dustbin	Rubbish is put into a **dustbin**.

Ff

fence	A **fence** is found round a garden or field.
fork	A **fork** has prongs. There are forks for eating food and for gardening.
freezer	A **freezer** keeps food frozen.
fridge	A **fridge** keeps food cold.

Gg

garage	A **garage** is where a car is kept.
garden	Plants grow in the **garden**.
gate	A **gate** is a way into a garden or field.

Hh

hall	The **hall** is the entrance to the house.

Ii

iron	A hot **iron** takes the creases out of our clothes.

Jj

jug	Liquids are poured from a **jug**.

33

The Home

Kk

kettle — Water is boiled in a **kettle**.

kitchen — The **kitchen** is the room where cooking is done.

knife — A **knife** is used to cut.

Ll

lamp — A **lamp** gives light.

letterbox — Letters and newspapers are pushed through the **letterbox**.

lounge — The **lounge** is the sitting room in the house.

Mm

mat — A **mat** is a small rug.

mattress — The **mattress** is the thick, soft part of a bed.

mirror — People look at themselves in a **mirror**.

Pp

pan — A **pan** is used for cooking.

plate — A **plate** is used to hold food.

plug — A **plug** keeps the water in a basin or bath.

porch — A **porch** is a covered entrance to a house.

The Home

Qq

quilt — A **quilt** keeps you warm in bed.

Rr

radiator — A **radiator** gives off heat.

roof — The **roof** is the cover of a house.

rug — A **rug** is a mat.

Ss

settee — A **settee** is a long seat.

shed — A **shed** is a wooden hut.

shower — The **shower** gives a spray of water to stand under.

sideboard — A **sideboard** is a piece of furniture.

sink — Dishes, pans and cutlery are washed in a **sink**.

spoon — A **spoon** is a piece of cutlery.

stairs — **Stairs** are used to get to rooms on another floor.

step — A **step** is often outside doors.

stool — A **stool** is a seat without a back and arms.

Tt

table — Meals are eaten at a **table**.

The Home

tap	A **tap** is turned on to get water.
teapot	Tea is made in a **teapot**.
telephone	People talk to each other on the **telephone**.
television	You can watch programmes on the **television**.
tiles	**Tiles** are used to cover roofs and walls.
tin opener	A **tin opener** is used to open tinned food.
toaster	Bread is put in a **toaster** to make toast.
toothbrush	A **toothbrush** is used to clean teeth.
towel	A **towel** is used to dry on after washing.
tumbledrier	A **tumbledrier** dries damp clothes.

Vv

vacuum cleaner	A **vacuum cleaner** collects dust and dirt.
vase	A **vase** holds flowers.

The Home

video recorder	A **video recorder** is used with the television set to show films and record programmes.

Ww

wall	A **wall** is the side of a building or room.

wardrobe	Clothes are kept in a **wardrobe**.

washbasin	The **washbasin** is used for washing hands and faces.

washer	A **washer** is used for washing dirty clothes.

window	A **window** lets in light to a room. You can open a window to let in fresh air.

Words about People

Aa

acrobat — An **acrobat** does clever tricks.

actor — An **actor** takes part in plays at the theatre, in films or on TV.

actress — An **actress** is a lady actor.

adult — An **adult** is a grown-up person.

air hostess — An **air hostess** looks after passengers on an aircraft.

architect — An **architect** plans new buildings.

artist — An **artist** draws and paints pictures.

astronaut — An **astronaut** travels in space in a spaceship.

athlete — An **athlete** takes part in sports.

audience — An **audience** is a crowd of people watching and listening to something.

aunt — An **aunt** is the sister of your mother or father, or the wife of your uncle.

author — An **author** writes books.

Bb

baby — A **baby** is a very young child.

People

baker	A **baker** bakes and sells bread, pies and cakes.
ballerina	A **ballerina** is a young lady dancer in the ballet.
barber	A **barber** cuts men's and boys' hair.
boy	A **boy** is a child who grows up to be a man.
bricklayer	A **bricklayer** uses bricks to build walls.
bride	A **bride** is a woman on her wedding day.
bridegroom	A **bridegroom** is a man on his wedding day.
brother	A boy is a **brother** to the other children of his father and mother.
builder	A **builder** builds houses and other buildings.
burglar	A **burglar** breaks into buildings and steals things.
butcher	A **butcher** sells meat.

Cc

captain	A **captain** is in charge of a ship or a sports team.

People

caretaker	A **caretaker** looks after a building such as a school.
chauffeur	A **chauffeur** is paid to drive a car.
chef	A **chef** is the head cook in a hotel or restaurant.
chemist	A **chemist** sells medicines.
children	**Children** are young girls and boys.
choir	A **choir** is a group of singers.
clerk	A **clerk** works in an office.
clown	A **clown** does funny things in the circus.
comedian	A **comedian** makes people laugh.
conductor	A **conductor** conducts a band or an orchestra.
cook	A **cook** cooks meals.
cousin	A **cousin** is the child of your aunt or uncle.
cowboy	A **cowboy** looks after cattle on a ranch.

People

crew	The **crew** are the people who work on a ship or an aircraft.
crowd	A **crowd** is a large number of people.
customer	A **customer** buys from a shop or store.

Dd

dad	**Dad** is another name for father.
daughter	A **daughter** is a girl child.
decorator	A **decorator** papers walls and paints houses.
dentist	A **dentist** looks after people's teeth.
detective	A **detective** is a policeman who tries to catch criminals.
disc jockey	A **disc jockey** plays records at a disco or on the radio.
diver	A **diver** works underwater.
doctor	A **doctor** takes care of sick people.
driver	A **driver** drives a car, bus, lorry or train.

People

dustbinman — A **dustbinman** takes away rubbish from houses.

Ee

editor — An **editor** is in charge of a newspaper.

electrician — An **electrician** repairs many kinds of electrical things.

engineer — An **engineer** makes or repairs engines and machines.

Ff

family — A mother and father and their children are a **family**.

farmer — A **farmer** grows crops and looks after animals on a farm.

fireman — A **fireman's** job is to put out fires.

fisherman — A **fisherman** catches fish in the sea.

florist — A **florist** sells flowers and plants.

friend — A **friend** is someone you know well and like.

Gg

giant — A **giant** is a very large person.

gipsy — A **gipsy** lives in a caravan and travels from place to place.

People

girl	A **girl** is a child who grows up to be a woman.
grandchild	You are a **grandchild** of your grandparents.
grandfather	Your **grandfather** is the father of your mum or dad.
grandmother	Your **grandmother** is the mother of your mum or dad.
grocer	A **grocer** sells goods in his shop.

Hh

hairdresser	A **hairdresser** takes care of people's hair.
headteacher	The **headteacher** is in charge of a school.
hero	A **hero** is a very brave boy or man.
heroine	A **heroine** is a very brave girl or woman.
husband	A **husband** is a man who is married.

Ii

infant	An **infant** is a very young child.

Jj

jockey	A **jockey** rides horses in races.
joiner	A **joiner** makes things out of wood.

People

judge	A **judge** sits in a law court.
juggler	A **juggler** does clever tricks throwing and catching things.

Kk
king	A **king** is the head man of a country.

Ll
lady	A **lady** is another name for a woman.
librarian	A **librarian** looks after books in a library.
lumberjack	A **lumberjack** cuts down trees in the forest.

Mm
magician	A **magician** does magic tricks.
manager	A **manager** is in charge of an office, a bank or a football club.
mason	A **mason** carves and builds with stone.
mayor	The **mayor** is the chief person of a town.
mechanic	A **mechanic** repairs machines and engines.

miner	A **miner** works underground.

People

monk	A **monk** is a man who lives in a monastery.
mother	**Mother** is another word for mum.
musician	A **musician** plays musical instruments.

Nn

neighbour	A **neighbour** lives near you.
nephew	A **nephew** is the son of a sister or brother.
newsagent	A **newsagent** sells newspapers and magazines.
newsreader	A **newsreader** reads the news on the radio or on T.V.
niece	A **niece** is the daughter of a sister or brother.
nun	A **nun** is a woman who lives in a convent.
nurse	A **nurse** looks after the sick, the old and the very young.

Oo

optician	An **optician** looks after people's eyes.

45

People

orphan	An **orphan** is a child who has no parents.
Pp	
passenger	A **passenger** rides in a plane, bus, train or car.
patient	A **patient** is someone being treated by a doctor or dentist.
pianist	A **pianist** plays the piano.
pilot	The **pilot** flies the aeroplane.
plumber	A **plumber** works with water pipes and taps.
police officer	A **police officer** keeps law and order.
porter	A **porter** carries luggage at an airport, hotel or station.
postman	A **postman** delivers letters and parcels.
priest	A **priest** is in charge of a church.
prince	A **prince** is the son of a king or queen.
princess	A **princess** is the daughter of a king or queen.

People

printer	A **printer** prints books, magazines and newspapers.
pupil	A **pupil** is taught in school.

Qq
queen	A **queen** is the head lady of a country.
queue	A **queue** is a line of people waiting.

Rr
rabbi	A **rabbi** is a Jewish leader.
ranger	A **ranger** looks after a forest, park or a game reserve.
referee	A **referee** is in charge of a game such as football.
reporter	A **reporter** writes for a newspaper.

Ss
sailor	A **sailor** works on a ship.
sculptor	A **sculptor** carves statues or shapes.
secretary	A **secretary** works in an office.
sentry	A **sentry** is a soldier who keeps guard.
shepherd	A **shepherd** looks after flocks of sheep.

People

sheriff	A **sheriff** keeps law and order in parts of U.S.A.
shopkeeper	A **shopkeeper** sells goods from a shop.
sister	A girl is a **sister** to other children of her father and mother.
soldier	A **soldier** is in the army and wears a uniform.
son	A **son** is a boy child.
surgeon	A **surgeon** is a doctor who does operations in hospital.

Tt

tailor	A **tailor** makes clothes.
teacher	A **teacher** teaches children in school.
teenager	A **teenager** is between 13 and 19 years of age.
traffic warden	A **traffic warden** makes sure that cars are parked in the right places.
tramp	A **tramp** wanders from place to place usually sleeping out of doors.
triplets	**Triplets** are three children born at the same time to one mother.

People

twins	**Twins** are two children born at the same time to one mother.
typist	A **typist** uses a typewriter in an office.

Uu
umpire	An **umpire** is in charge of a game such as tennis and cricket.
uncle	An **uncle** is the brother of your father or mother or the husband of your aunt.

Vv
ventriloquist	A **ventriloquist** seems to be able to make a puppet speak.
vet	A **vet** takes care of sick animals.
vicar	A **vicar** is in charge of a church.

Ww
waiter	A **waiter** is a man who serves food in a restaurant.
waitress	A **waitress** is a woman who serves food in a restaurant.
wife	A **wife** is a woman who is married.
witch	A **witch** is a woman who is supposed to make magic.
wizard	A **wizard** is a man who is supposed to make magic.

The Body

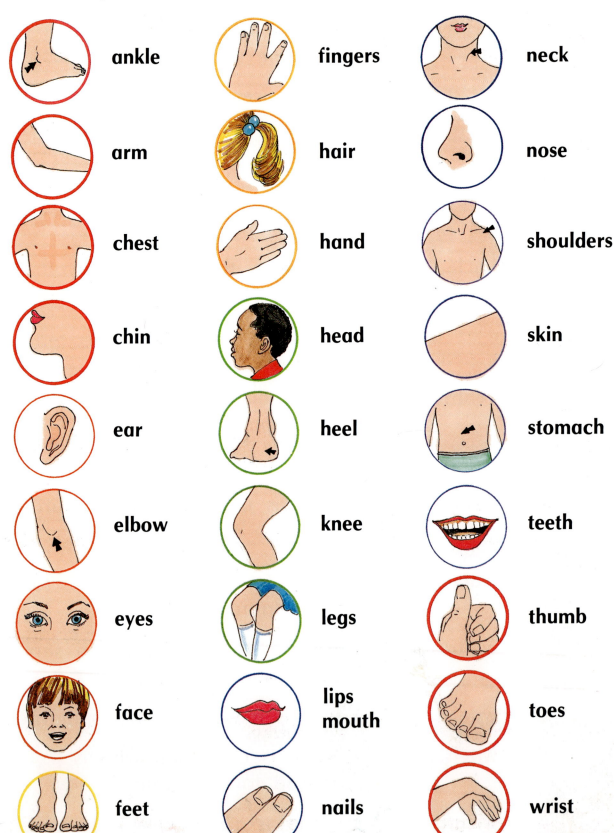

Clothes

 anorak

 coat

 jodhpurs

apron

 dress

 jumper

belt

 dressing gown

 kilt

bikini

 duffel coat

 leotard

 blouse

 football boots

 mittens

 bonnet

 gloves

 moccasins

 boots

 hat

 nightdress

 cap

 jacket

 overalls

 cardigan

 jeans

 pants

Clothes

 plimsolls
 skirt
 tights

 pullover
 slippers
 tracksuit

pyjamas
 socks
 trainers

 raincoat
 stockings
 trousers

 sandals
 suit
 trunks

 scarf
 sweater
 T. shirt

 shirt
 sweatshirt
 underpants

 shoes
 swimsuit
 vest

 shorts
 tie
 wellingtons

Food and Drink

Aa

apple — The **apple** is a fruit grown on a tree.

apricot — The **apricot** is a fruit. It is small, round and juicy.

Bb

bacon — **Bacon** is meat from the pig.

banana — A **banana** is a long, curved fruit with a thick yellow skin.

barbecue — A **barbecue** is a meal cooked outside over hot charcoal.

beef — **Beef** is the meat from a cow or bull.

beer — **Beer** is a strong drink made from hops and barley.

beetroot — The **beetroot** has a dark, red, round root which is boiled and eaten.

biscuits — **Biscuits** are made with flour, sugar and fat. They are sweet and crispy.

blackberries — **Blackberries** are small and juicy. They often grow in hedgerows.

blackcurrants — **Blackcurrants** are small, black fruits that grow on a small bush.

blancmange — A **blancmange** is a kind of jelly made with milk.

Food and Drink

bread — **Bread** is made with flour and baked in an oven.

breakfast — **Breakfast** is the first meal of the day.

broccoli — **Broccoli** is a kind of small cauliflower.

butter — **Butter** is soft and yellow, and is made from cream.

Cc

cabbage — A **cabbage** is a vegetable with thick, green leaves.

cake — A **cake** is a sweet food made from flour, sugar and fat, and baked in an oven.

carrots — **Carrots** have long, orange-coloured roots which are eaten.

cauliflower — A **cauliflower** is a vegetable with a white part in the middle.

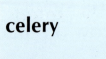

celery — **Celery** has long, white stems which are eaten.

cereals — **Cereals** are usually eaten at breakfast.

cheese — **Cheese** is made from milk.

Food and Drink

cherries — **Cherries** are small, round fruits grown on cherry trees.

chips — **Chips** are thin pieces of fried potato.

chocolate — **Chocolate** is a sweet made from cocoa, sugar and milk.

cider — **Cider** is a strong drink made from apple juice.

cocoa — **Cocoa** is the brown powder made from the beans of the cacao tree.

coconut — A **coconut** is a very large, hard-shelled nut. The white lining is eaten.

coffee — **Coffee** is a hot drink made from the roasted seeds of the coffee bush.

cola — **Cola** is a sweet, fizzy drink.

cream — **Cream** is the thick part of milk.

cress — **Cress** is used in salads.

crisps — **Crisps** are very thin slices of fried potato.

cucumber — A **cucumber** is a vegetable eaten in a salad.

Food and Drink

currants — **Currants** are small dried grapes.

curry — **Curry** is hot, spicy food.

custard — **Custard** is a thick, sweet sauce which is put on puddings and tarts.

Dd

damson — A **damson** is a small plum.

date — A **date** is a small, sticky sweet fruit.

dessert — A **dessert** is sweet food eaten after the main part of the meal.

dinner — **Dinner** is the main meal of the day.

doughnut — A **doughnut** is a small, round cake. It is fried and dipped in sugar.

Ee

Easter egg — An **Easter egg** is made of chocolate.

egg — An **egg** is laid by a hen.

Ff

fig — A **fig** is a soft, sweet fruit with many seeds.

fishcake — A **fishcake** is a small, round, flat cake made of cooked fish and potato.

fish finger — A **fish finger** is a thin piece of fish covered in breadcrumbs.

Food and Drink

flour — **Flour** is a fine powder made by grinding grain such as wheat.

Gg

gooseberries — **Gooseberries** are small fruit with hairy skins.

grapes — **Grapes** are small, round fruits which grow in bunches on vines.

gravy — **Gravy** is a sauce usually made with the juice of cooked meat.

Hh

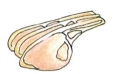

ham — **Ham** is meat from the leg of a pig.

hamburger — A **hamburger** is round and is made of minced meat and spices.

hot dog — A **hot dog** is a hot sausage inside a bread roll.

Ii

ice cream — **Ice cream** is a favourite cold sweet.

icing — **Icing** is used to cover cakes.

Jj

jam — **Jam** is fruit boiled with sugar.

jelly — **Jelly** is a cold, fruity sweet often eaten at parties.

juice — **Juice** is the liquid in fruits and vegetables.

Food and Drink

Ll

lamb — **Lamb** is the meat of young sheep.

leek — A **leek** has a white stem and long green leaves. It tastes like an onion.

lemon — A **lemon** has a sour taste.

lemonade — **Lemonade** is a drink made from lemon juice, water and sugar.

lettuce — A **lettuce** has large leaves and is eaten in salads.

lollipop — A **lollipop** is a large sweet on a stick for licking.

Mm

margarine — **Margarine** is often used instead of butter.

marmalade — **Marmalade** is usually eaten at breakfast. It is made of oranges or lemons.

meat — **Meat** comes from animals. We buy it at the butchers.

melon — A **melon** is a large sweet juicy fruit.

milk — Cows give us **milk**.

mince — **Mince** is meat chopped up into very small pieces.

Food and Drink

mincemeat	**Mincemeat** is chopped up fruit, nuts and spices.
mushroom	A **mushroom** is a vegetable.
mutton	**Mutton** is the meat of sheep.

Nn

nuts	**Nuts** are fruits or seeds with hard shells.

Oo

oats	**Oats** is a cereal used to make porridge.
omelette	An **omelette** is made from fried, beaten eggs.
onion	An **onion** is a tasty vegetable.
orange	An **orange** is a round, juicy, sweet fruit.

Pp

pancake	A **pancake** is cooked in a frying pan. It is made from eggs, flour and milk.
pastry	**Pastry** is the crust of pies and tarts.
peach	A **peach** is a sweet, juicy fruit with a soft skin.
pear	A **pear** is a juicy fruit.

Food and Drink

peas — **Peas** grow in a pod.

picnic — A **picnic** is a meal eaten outside usually on a trip.

pie — A **pie** is fruit or meat baked in pastry.

pineapple — A **pineapple** is a large, sweet, juicy fruit.

pizza — A **pizza** is cheese, tomatoes and other foods cooked on pastry.

plum — A **plum** is a small, soft fruit with a stone in the middle.

pork — **Pork** is meat that comes from a pig.

porridge — **Porridge** is oats boiled in water or milk. It is usually eaten at breakfast.

potato — The **potato** is a vegetable grown under the ground. Potatoes can be baked, boiled or fried.

pudding — A **pudding** is a sweet food eaten at the end of a meal.

Rr

radish — A **radish** is eaten raw in salad.

raisin — A **raisin** is a dried grape.

Food and Drink

	raspberries	**Raspberries** are sweet, soft red berries.
	rhubarb	The thick stalks of the **rhubarb** plant are cooked with sugar.
	rice	**Rice** is a grain. It is cooked before it is eaten.

Ss

	salad	A **salad** is a mixture of vegetables which is eaten cold.
	salt	**Salt** is used in cooking and eating.
	sandwich	A **sandwich** is made from two pieces of bread with some food between them.
	sauce	**Sauce** is a liquid to improve the taste of food.
	sausage	A **sausage** is chopped meat in a skin.
	snack	A **snack** is a small, quick meal.
	soup	**Soup** is made from meat or fish or vegetables and water.
	spaghetti	**Spaghetti** is long strings of pasta boiled in water.

Food and Drink

spices — **Spices** are used to improve the taste of food.

sprouts — **Sprouts** look like tiny cabbages.

steak — A **steak** is a thick slice of fish or meat.

stew — **Stew** is meat and vegetables boiled slowly.

strawberry — A **strawberry** is a small, soft, juicy fruit.

sugar — **Sugar** is used to sweeten food and drinks.

supper — **Supper** is the last meal of the day.

sweets — **Sweets** are made of sugar and often chocolate.

syrup — **Syrup** is a thick, sweet, sticky liquid.

Tt

tangerine — A **tangerine** is like a small orange.

tart — A **tart** is pastry filled with jam or fruit.

tea — **Tea** is a hot drink made by pouring boiling water on dried tea leaves.

Food and Drink

toast — **Toast** is bread that is heated until it is crisp and brown.

tomato — A **tomato** is a soft fruit, often eaten in a salad.

treacle — **Treacle** is a dark syrup.

trifle — A **trifle** is made of sponge cake, custard, fruit and cream.

turnip — A **turnip** is a round vegetable and can be white or yellow.

Vv

veal — **Veal** is the meat of a calf.

vegetable — A **vegetable** is any plant other than fruit used for food.

Ww

water — **Water** is the most important liquid of all.

wheat — **Wheat** is made into flour and breakfast foods.

wine — **Wine** is a strong drink made from the juices of grapes or other fruit.

Yy

yoghurt — **Yoghurt** is a thick, creamy food made from milk.

Words about Plants

Aa

acorn — An **acorn** is the seed of the oak tree.

Bb

beech — The **beech** is a large tree with dark, shiny leaves.

blossom — **Blossom** is the flowers of plants and trees.

bluebell — The **bluebell** is a spring flower which grows in woods.

bulb — Some flowers grow from a **bulb**.

buttercup — The **buttercup** is a small yellow wild flower.

Cc

cactus — A **cactus** is a prickly plant.

carnation — A **carnation** is a sweet-smelling flower.

catkin — The **catkin** is the fluffy flower of some trees.

cedar — The **cedar** is a tall, evergreen tree.

chestnut — The **chestnut** is a large tree.

clover — A **clover** is a small wild plant.

Plants

conker	A **conker** is the nut of the horse-chestnut tree.
corn	**Corn** is the seeds of wheat, barley, oats and maize used as food.
cotton	**Cotton** is the soft white hairs of the cotton plant.
crocus	The **crocus** is a small spring flower.

Dd
daffodil	The **daffodil** is a spring flower.
daisy	The **daisy** is a small, wild flower.
dandelion	The **dandelion** is a wild plant with yellow flowers.

Ee
elm	The **elm** is a large tree.

Ff
fern	A **fern** has feathery leaves but no flowers.
fir	The **fir** tree is evergreen and has cones.
flower	A **flower** is coloured blossom of a plant.
forest	A **forest** is where a very large number of trees grow.

65

Plants

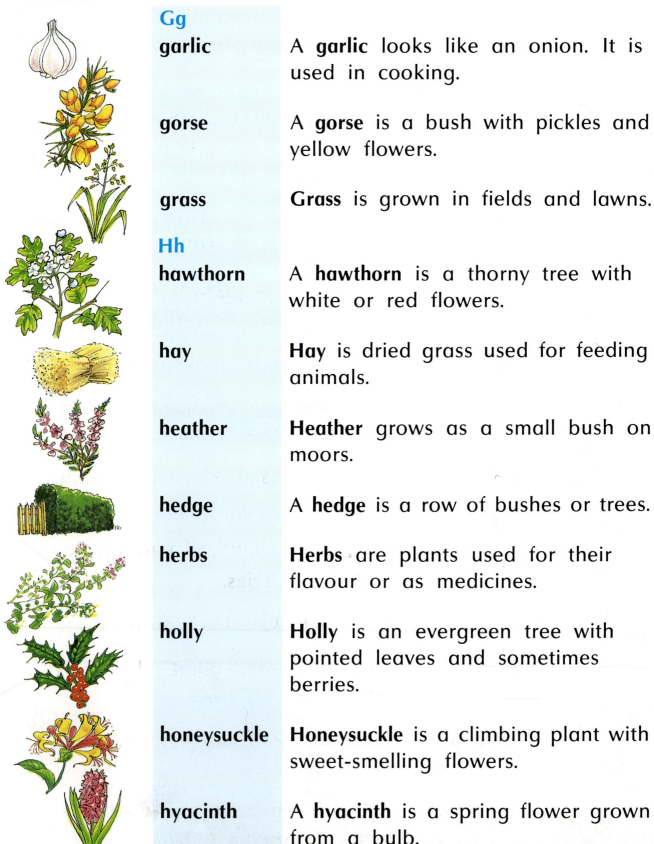

Gg

garlic	A **garlic** looks like an onion. It is used in cooking.
gorse	A **gorse** is a bush with pickles and yellow flowers.
grass	**Grass** is grown in fields and lawns.

Hh

hawthorn	A **hawthorn** is a thorny tree with white or red flowers.
hay	**Hay** is dried grass used for feeding animals.
heather	**Heather** grows as a small bush on moors.
hedge	A **hedge** is a row of bushes or trees.
herbs	**Herbs** are plants used for their flavour or as medicines.
holly	**Holly** is an evergreen tree with pointed leaves and sometimes berries.
honeysuckle	**Honeysuckle** is a climbing plant with sweet-smelling flowers.
hyacinth	A **hyacinth** is a spring flower grown from a bulb.

Plants

Ii

ivy — **Ivy** is an evergreen climbing plant.

Ll

laburnum — The **laburnum** is a small tree with long, yellow flowers. Its seeds are poisonous.

larch — The **larch** is a tall tree with cones and long thin leaves.

lavender — **Lavender** is a plant with sweet-smelling flowers.

leaf — A **leaf** is part of a plant or tree.

lilac — The **lilac** is a small tree having sweet-smelling blossom.

lupin — The **lupin** is a tall garden plant.

Mm

maize — **Maize** is a kind of corn grown in warm countries.

marigold — The **marigold** is a garden flower.

mint — **Mint** is a small plant. Its leaves have a strong taste.

mistletoe — **Mistletoe** is an evergreen plant with white berries.

mushroom — A **mushroom** does not have any roots. It can be eaten.

Plants

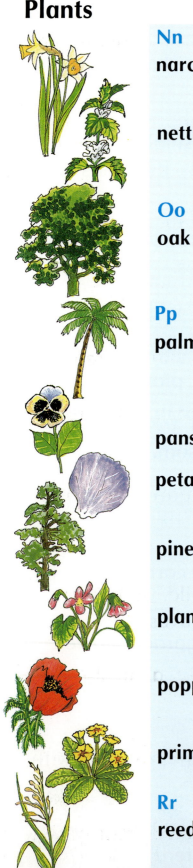

Nn
narcissus — A **narcissus** is a spring flower grown from a bulb.

nettle — The **nettle** grows wild. Its leaves can sting.

Oo
oak — The **oak** is a large tree with hard wood.

Pp
palm — The **palm** is a tall tree which grows in hot lands. Its leaves are long and flat.

pansy — The **pansy** is a small garden flower.

petal — A **petal** is one of the coloured parts of a flower.

pine — The **pine** is a tall evergreen tree with cones.

plant — A **plant** grows in the ground or in water.

poppy — The **poppy** is a brightly coloured flower.

primrose — The **primrose** is a yellow, wild flower.

Rr
reed — The **reed** is a tall grass that grows near water. It has a hollow stem.

Plants

roots	**Roots** are the parts of a plant that are in the soil.
rose	A **rose** is a flower that grows on a thorny bush.

Ss

seaweed	**Seaweed** is a plant that grows in the sea.
seed	A plant grows from a **seed**.
shrub	A **shrub** is a small, bushy tree.
sunflower	The **sunflower** is a tall plant with large yellow flowers.
sycamore	The **sycamore** is a tree with large leaves.

Tt

thistle	The **thistle** grows wild. It has a prickly stem and leaves.
toadstool	A **toadstool** looks like a mushroom. It is poisonous.
tree	A **tree** is a large plant with a trunk, branches and leaves.
tulip	A **tulip** is a spring flower that grows from a bulb.

Plants

twig — A **twig** is a very small branch on a tree or bush.

Vv

vine — A **vine** is a climbing plant. Grapes grow on a vine.

violet — The **violet** is a small plant that flowers in spring.

Ww

weed — A **weed** is a wild plant that grows in places where it is not wanted.

willow — The **willow** is a large tree with thin branches that bend.

Yy

yew — The **yew** is an evergreen tree.

Words about Transport

Aa

aeroplane	An **aeroplane** flies in the sky.
airliner	An **airliner** carries passengers.
ambulance	An **ambulance** takes sick and injured people to hospital.

Bb

barge	A **barge** carries goods on rivers and canals.
bicycle	A **bicycle** has two wheels, two pedals and handlebars.
boat	A **boat** is used on water.
bulldozer	A **bulldozer** is used to move loads of earth.
bus	A **bus** carries people who pay to travel on it.

Cc

cable car	A **cable car** carries people up and down mountains.
canoe	A **canoe** is a light, narrow boat moved with a paddle.
capsule	The **capsule** is the cabin of a spaceship.
car	A **car** is used by people to drive from place to place.

Transport

caravan — A **caravan** is a small house on wheels, usually pulled by a car.

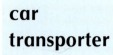

car transporter — Cars are carried on a **car transporter**.

coach — A **coach** is a bus which carries people on trips.

crane — Heavy things can be lifted and moved by a **crane**.

Dd

dinghy — A **dinghy** is a small sailing boat.

drifter — A **drifter** is a type of fishing boat.

Ee

engine — An **engine** pulls coaches and wagons on the railway.

escalator — An **escalator** is a moving staircase.

Ff

ferry — A **ferry** carries people and vehicles across a river or a narrow strip of water.

fire engine — A **fire engine** carries firemen and equipment to a fire.

freighter — A **freighter** is a ship that carries goods across the seas.

Gg

galleon — A **galleon** was an old sailing ship.

Transport

glider — A **glider** is an aeroplane without an engine.

gondola — A **gondola** is a small boat used on the canals of Venice.

Hh

hang glider — A **hang glider** looks like a large kite.

helicopter — A **helicopter** does not have wings. The blades go round to make it fly.

hovercraft — A **hovercraft** travels over water or land on a cushion of air.

hydrofoil — A **hydrofoil** travels quickly over the water on skis.

Jj

jeep — A **jeep** can travel across rough ground.

jet plane — A **jet plane** travels very fast.

juggernaut — A **juggernaut** is a very large lorry that travels long distances.

junk — A **junk** is a Chinese sailing ship.

Kk

kayak — A **kayak** is a canoe used by Eskimos.

Ll

launch — A **launch** is a large motor boat.

73

Transport

	**lifeboat**	A **lifeboat** is used to save people from drowning.
	lift	A **lift** carries people and things up and down in a building.
	lightship	A **lightship** is a small ship with a flashing light to warn other ships of danger.
	liner	A **liner** is a large ship which carries many people.
	**lorry**	A **lorry** carries big loads.

Mm

mail van — A **mail van** carries letters and parcels.

minibus — A **minibus** is like a large van with seats for about ten people.

module — A **module** is part of a spacecraft.

monorail — A **monorail** is a train which travels fast on one rail.

moped — A **moped** is a bicycle with a small engine.

motorboat — A **motorboat** is a small boat with an engine.

Transport

motorcycle — A **motorcycle** can travel at fast speeds.

Nn
narrow boat — A **narrow boat** is used on canals.

Pp
panda car — A **panda car** is used by the police.

parachute — A **parachute** is used by people to jump safely from an aircraft.

pram — Babies and young children are pushed in a **pram**.

Rr
raft — A **raft** is logs or planks tied together to make a kind of boat.

railway — A **railway** is a track for trains to run on.

rocket — A **rocket** is used to send space vehicles into space

rowing boat — A **rowing boat** is a small boat moved by using oars.

Ss
scooter — A **scooter** has two wheels and an engine.

ship — A **ship** is a large boat which sails on the sea.

Transport

sky lab	A **sky lab** is a space station in orbit round the earth.
sledge	A **sledge** slides over the ice and snow.
spaceship	A **spaceship** carries astronauts in space.
space shuttle	A **space shuttle** can travel between earth and space and land back on earth.
speedboat	A **speedboat** is a very fast motorboat.
stagecoach	A **stagecoach** was pulled by horses and carried people and baggage.
submarine	A **submarine** is a ship that can travel under water.
surfboard	A **surfboard** is a shaped board used for riding the large waves.

Tt

tank	A **tank** travels on tracks. It carries guns.
tanker	A **tanker** is a ship or lorry which carries liquids such as petrol and oil.

Transport

taxi	A **taxi** is a car that people pay to ride in.
tractor	A **tractor** pulls farm machines.
traffic	**Traffic** is everything that moves by land, sea or air.
trailer	A **trailer** is pulled by another vehicle.
train	A **train** runs on rails and carries people and goods.
tram	A **tram** is a kind of bus that runs on lines on a road.
trawler	A **trawler** is a fishing boat which drags a net along the sea bed.
tricycle	A **tricycle** is a three-wheeled cycle.
tug	A **tug** is a powerful boat which can push or pull large ships.

Vv
van — A **van** carries small loads.

Ww
warship — A **warship** is a powerful ship which carries weapons.

Yy
yacht — A **yacht** is a sailing ship.

Other Words — All Sorts

Aa

	air	**Air** is what we breathe.
	album	Stamps or photographs are kept in an **album.**
	anchor	An **anchor** is dropped in the sea to stop a ship moving.
	aquarium	Fish and other animals are kept in an **aquarium.**
	atlas	An **atlas** is a book of maps.
	avalanche	An **avalanche** is a huge fall of snow and rocks sliding down a mountain.

Bb

	badge	A **badge** shows that a person belongs to a school or club.
	bag	A **bag** is a container for carrying things.
	ball	A **ball** is round and used to play games.
	ballet	**Ballet** is a kind of dancing.
	balloon	A **balloon** floats in the air when blown up.
	band	People play music in a **band.**

78

All Sorts

basket	A **basket** is made of cane and is used for carrying things.
bat	A **bat** is used to hit a ball in games.
battery	A **battery** contains electricity to make things work.
bench	A **bench** is a long seat.
Bible	The **Bible** is the holy book of Christians.
blackboard	Teacher writes on a **blackboard.**
blizzard	A **blizzard** is a snowstorm.
book	A **book** is to read.
box	A **box** is used to hold things.

Cc

calculator	A **calculator** is used to work out sums.
camera	A **camera** is used to take photographs.
can	A **can** is a container made of tin.
canal	A **canal** is a waterway made by people.

All Sorts

candle	A **candle** is made of wax.
case	A **case** is used to carry clothes when people go away.
cash	**Cash** is another name for money.
cassette recorder	A **cassette recorder** plays tapes.
cello	A **cello** is a large musical instrument. It has strings.
chalk	**Chalk** is used to write on a blackboard.
chisel	A **chisel** is a tool to cut wood or stone.
circle	A **circle** is round like a ring.
class	A **class** is a group of children in a school.
clean	**Clean** means washed, not dirty.
cloud	A **cloud** floats in the sky. Tiny drops of water make a cloud.
coal	**Coal** is burned to give heat.
coin	A **coin** is a piece of money.

All Sorts

cold	Ice is **cold.**
comb	A **comb** is used to keep hair tidy.
computer	A **computer** is a machine which stores information and gives answers.
crayon	A **crayon** is like a wax pencil.

Dd

dam	A **dam** is a wall to hold back water.
dark	It is **dark** at night.
diamond	The **diamond** is a precious stone.
diary	A **diary** is a book of daily happenings.
dirty	**Dirty** means not clean.
disco	People dance to records at a **disco.**
doll	A **doll** is a toy baby.
drill	A **drill** is a tool used to make holes.
drizzle	**Drizzle** is very light rain.
drought	**Drought** is when there is no rain and water is scarce.

All Sorts

dry — Dry means not wet or damp.

Ee

earrings — Earrings are worn on the ears.

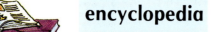

earthquake — An **earthquake** is a shaking of the earth.

east — **East** is where the sun rises.

encyclopedia — An **encyclopedia** is a book or set of books full of information.

envelope — A letter is put inside an **envelope.**

Ff

feathers — **Feathers** cover a bird's body.

felt-tip — A **felt-tip** is a kind of pen used for colouring.

film — A **film** is a moving picture and can be seen at the cinema.

fire — **Fire** is something burning and feels hot.

fireworks — **Fireworks** are made of gunpowder. They give off pretty sparks and loud bangs.

flag — Each country has a **flag** with its own pattern.

82

All Sorts

fleece	A **fleece** is the woolly coat of a sheep.
fog	**Fog** is thick, damp air. It is hard to see through.
football	**Football** is a game played by two teams.
funny	**Funny** things make people laugh.

Gg

gale	A **gale** is a very strong wind.
gas	**Gas** is used for cooking and heating.
glass	**Glass** is used in windows.
glasses	**Glasses** can help people to see better.
glue	**Glue** is used to stick things together.
gold	**Gold** is a very precious metal. Rings are made of gold.
greenhouse	A **greenhouse** is made of glass. Flowers and plants are grown inside.
guitar	A **guitar** is a musical instrument with strings.

All Sorts

gun	A **gun** is a weapon that fires bullets.

Hh

hail	**Hail** is frozen rain.
hair drier	A **hair drier** blows hot air to dry damp hair.
hammer	A **hammer** is a tool used for hitting things such as nails.
handbag	A **handbag** is a small bag for carrying things.
handkerchief	A **handkerchief** is used to wipe the nose.
happy	**Happy** means pleased and full of joy.
harp	A **harp** is a large musical instrument which stands on the floor. It is played by plucking the strings.
headphones	**Headphones** are used to listen to cassettes and records.
helmet	A **helmet** is worn to protect the head.
hoe	A **hoe** is a garden tool used for loosening the soil.

84

All Sorts

hose	A **hose** is a pipe used to water the garden and wash the car.
hot	**Hot** is very, very warm like fire.

Ii

ice	**Ice** is frozen water.
iceberg	An **iceberg** is a huge piece of ice floating in the sea.
ice skates	**Ice skates** have blades to help you glide over the ice.

Jj

jigsaw	Pieces of **jigsaw** fit together to make a picture.

Kk

kite	A **kite** is a toy which flies in the wind.

Ll

ladder	A **ladder** is used to reach high places.
lightning	**Lightning** is a flash of light in the sky when there is a storm.
little	**Little** means small.

long	**Long** is the opposite of short.

Mm

map	People use a **map** to find their way.

85

All Sorts

matches — **Matches** are used to light fires. You must not play with matches.

measles — **Measles** is an illness. Red spots cover the body.

medicine — **Medicine** is taken by sick people to help them get well.

microphone — A **microphone** makes the voice sound much louder.

money — **Money** buys things.

moon — The **moon** shines in the sky at night.

mower — A **mower** is used to cut grass.

mumps — **Mumps** is an illness. The neck and face swell and the throat hurts.

Nn

nails — **Nails** are the hard part at the end of the fingers.

needles — **Needles** are used for sewing and knitting.

new — **New** is something just made or bought.

Oo

oars — **Oars** are used to row a boat.

All Sorts

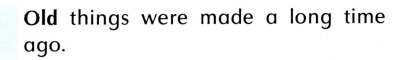

old	**Old** things were made a long time ago.
orchestra	An **orchestra** is a large number of musicians playing together.
organ	An **organ** is a musical instrument that looks like a piano.

Pp

paddle	A **paddle** is a short oar used to move a canoe.
paint	**Paint** is used to colour things.
paper	People write, draw and paint on **paper.**
party	A **party** is when a number of people get together and have a good time.
pebbles	**Pebbles** are small stones often found on a beach.
pencil	A **pencil** is used for writing and drawing.
petrol	**Petrol** is used to drive car engines.
photograph	A **photograph** is a picture taken by a camera.

All Sorts

piano	A **piano** is a musical instrument with black and white keys.
postbox	Letters are posted in a **postbox.**
puppet	A **puppet** is a kind of doll whose arms and legs can be moved.
purse	Money is carried in a **purse.**

Rr

racket	A **racket** is a bat used in tennis, squash and badminton.
radio	People listen to music and news on the **radio.**
rain	**Rain** is water falling in drops from clouds.
rainbow	A **rainbow** is made by the sun shining through light rain.
recorder	A **recorder** is a musical instrument played by blowing.
record player	Records are played on a **record player.**
ring	A **ring** is worn on a finger.
roller skates	**Roller skates** have small wheels and fit on the feet.

All Sorts

rope — A **rope** is a thick cord used for tying things.

rounders — **Rounders** is a game played with a bat and ball.

rubber — A **rubber** is used to rub out pencil lines.

ruler — A **ruler** is used for drawing straight lines and measuring.

Ss

saddle — A **saddle** is a seat for a rider of a horse or cycle.

sand — **Sand** is tiny grains of rock which makes the beach.

saw — A **saw** can cut through wood.

scales — **Scales** are used to weigh things.

scissors — **Scissors** cut through cloth and paper.

screwdriver — A **screwdriver** turns screws.

shears — **Shears** are used to cut hedges and grass.

signpost — A **signpost** helps drivers to find their way.

All Sorts

sleet	**Sleet** is rain mixed with snow.
snow	**Snow** is soft, white flakes of frozen water that fall in cold weather.
snowball	A **snowball** is a ball made of snow.
snowman	A **snowman** is a figure of man made from snow.

soil	**Soil** is the ground in which plants grow.
spade	A **spade** is a tool used for digging.
stamp	A **stamp** is stuck on a letter to send it through the post.
stars	**Stars** shine in the sky at night.
sun	The **sun** gives the earth light and heat.

Tt

tall	**Tall** means high.
television	A **television** set has a screen which shows pictures.
thin	**Thin** means not thick or fat.

thunder	**Thunder** is the loud noise heard in a storm.

All Sorts

	toothpaste	**Toothpaste** keeps your teeth clean.
	torch	A **torch** is a light carried in the hand.
	trapeze	Acrobats swing on a **trapeze** in a circus.
	trumpet	A **trumpet** is a musical instrument played by blowing.
	typewriter	A **typewriter** prints letters and numbers on paper.
	tyre	A **tyre** is a rubber ring round the outside of a wheel.

Uu
umbrella — An **umbrella** keeps off the rain.

Vv
video recorder — A **video recorder** plays tapes which show pictures on the T.V. screen.

violin — A **violin** is a musical instrument with strings. It is played with a bow.

Ww
wallet — A **wallet** can hold money, papers and photographs.

war — **War** is when two or more countries fight each other.

All Sorts

watering can   A **watering can** is used to pour water on plants in the garden or in the house.

wedding   A **wedding** is when a man and woman are married.

wheel   A **wheel** is a ring of metal which turns and helps things move more easily.

wheelbarrow   A **wheelbarrow** is a little cart used to carry small loads.

wind   **Wind** is air moving quickly.

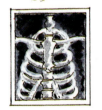

wool   **Wool** is the soft, thick hair of sheep and lambs.

Xx

x ray   An **x ray** gives doctors a picture of the inside of a body.

xylophone   A **xylophone** is a musical instrument made of bars of wood which are hit with a hammer.

Yy

yo yo   A **yo yo** is a toy which moves up and down a string.

Zz

zip   A **zip** is a fastener with a sliding catch.

Where

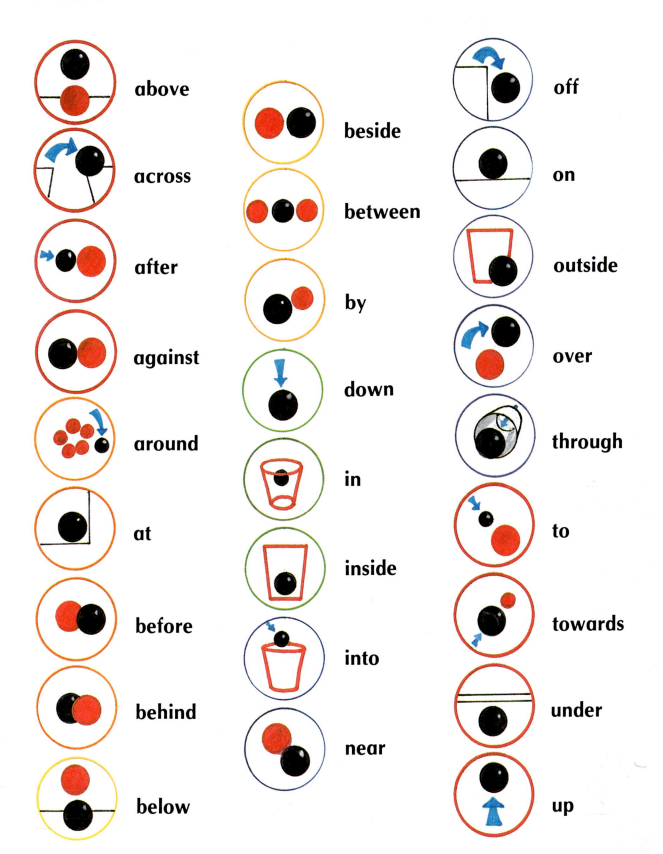

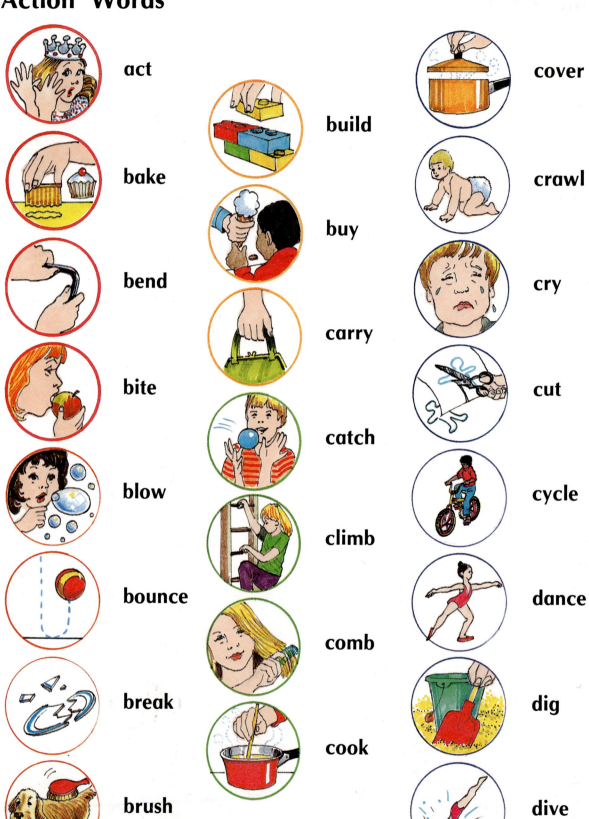

Action Words

 draw

 dress

 drink

 drive

 drop

 eat

 fall

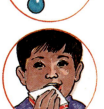 feed

 fight

 fill

 fly

 gather

 give

 help

 hide

 hit

 hold

 hop

 iron

 jump

 kick

 kiss

 knit

95

Action Words

knock
laugh
lie
lift
make
meet
mend
mix

mow
open
paint
pat
pick
plant
play

pour
print
pull
push
rake
read
ride
roll

Action Words

Colours

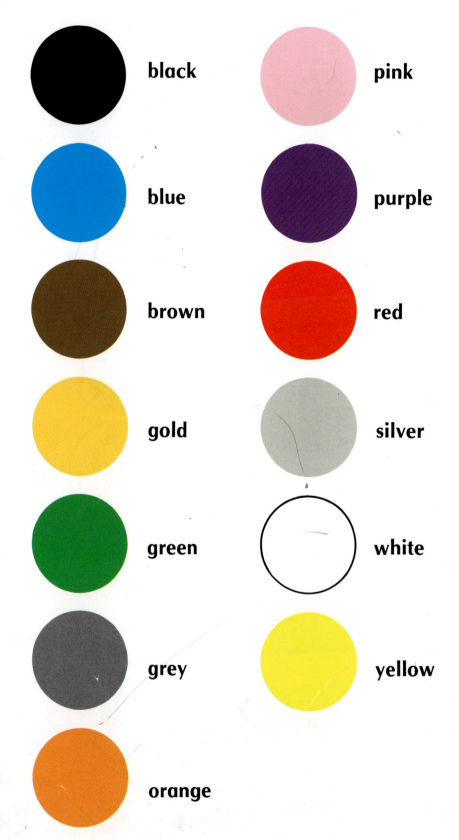

Numbers

1	one	20	twenty	1st	first
2	two	30	thirty	2nd	second
3	three	40	forty	3rd	third
4	four	50	fifty	4th	fourth
5	five	60	sixty	5th	fifth
6	six	70	seventy	6th	sixth
7	seven	80	eighty	7th	seventh
8	eight	90	ninety	8th	eighth
9	nine	100	one hundred	9th	ninth
10	ten	1000	one thousand	10th	tenth

Months of the Year

January
February
March
April
May
June
July
August
September
October
November
December

Days of the Week

Sunday					
Monday					
Tuesday					
Wednesday					
Thursday					
Friday					
Saturday					

Seasons

Spring

Autumn

Summer

Winter

Time

second
minute
hour

day
week
month
year

today
yesterday
tomorrow

morning
afternoon
night

INDEX

Aa
abbey 19
above 93
acorn 64
acrobat 38
across 93
act 94
actor 38
actress 38
adult 38
aerial 31
aeroplane 71
after 93
afternoon 101
against 93
air 78
air hostess 38
airliner 71
airport 19
album 78
alligator 2
Alsatian 2
ambulance 71
amphibian 2
anchor 78
animal 2
ankle 50
anorak 51
ant 2
antelope 2
apartment 19
apple 53
apricot 53
April 100
apron 51
aquarium 78
architect 38
arm 50
armchair 31
around 93
artist 38
astronaut 38
at 93
athlete 38
atlas 78
audience 38
August 100
aunt 38
author 38
Autumn 101
avalanche 78
aviary 19

Bb
baby 38
bacon 53
badge 78
badger 2
bag 78
bake 94
baker 39
bakery 19
ball 78
ballerina 39
ballet 78
balloon 78
banana 53
band 78
barbecue 53
barber 39
barge 71
barn 19
basket 79
bat 2, 79
bath 31
bathroom 31
battery 79
bay 19
beach 19
bear 2
beaver 2
bed 31
bee 3
beech 64
beef 53
beer 53
beetle 3
beetroot 53
before 93
behind 93
below 93
belt 51
bench 79
bend 94
beside 93
between 93
Bible 79
bicycle 71
bikini 51
bird 3
biscuits 53
bite 94
black 98
blackberries 53
blackbird 3
blackboard 79
blackcurrants 53
blancmange 53
blanket 31
blizzard 79
blossom 64
blouse 51
blow 94
blue 98
bluebell 64
blue tit 3
boat 71
bonnet 51
book 79
bookcase 31
boots 51
bounce 94
boutique 19
box 79
boy 39
bread 54
break 94
breakfast 54
bricklayer 39
bricks 31
bride 39
bridegroom 39
bridge 19
broccoli 54
brother 39
brown 98
brush 31, 94
bucket 31
budgerigar 3
buffalo 3
build 94
builder 39
bulb 64
bull 3
bulldog 3
bulldozer 71
bungalow 19
burglar 39
bus 71
bus station 20
butcher 39
butter 54
buttercup 64
butterfly 3
buy 94
by 93

Cc
cabbage 54
cabin 20
cable car 71
cactus 64
café 20
cage 20
cake 54
calculator 79
calf 3
camel 3
camera 79
camp 20
can 79
canal 20, 79
canary 4
candle 80
canoe 71
cap 51
capsule 71
captain 39
car 71
caravan 72
cardigan 51
caretaker 40
carnation 64
car park 20
carpet 31
carrots 54
carry 94
car transporter 72
case 80
cash 80
cassette recorder 80
castle 20
cat 4
catch 94
caterpillar 4
cathedral 20
catkin 64
cattle 4
cauliflower 54
cave 20
cedar 64
ceiling 31
celery 54
cell 20
cellar 20
cello 80
centipede 4
cereals 54
chair 31
chalk 80
chameleon 4
chapel 21
chauffeur 40
cheese 54
cheetah 4
chef 40
chemist 40
cherries 55
chest 50
chestnut 64
chicken 4
children 40
chimney 32
chimpanzee 4
chin 50
chips 55
chisel 80
chocolate 55
choir 40
church 21
cider 55
cinema 21
circle 80
circus 21
city 21
class 80
classroom 21
clean 80
clerk 40
cliff 21
climb 94
clinic 21
clock 32
cloud 80
clover 64
clown 40
coach 72
coal 80
coast 21
coat 51
cobra 4
cocoa 55
coconut 55
coffee 55
coin 80
cola 55
cold 81
comb 81, 94
comedian 40
computer 81
conductor 40
conker 65
cook 40, 94
cooker 32
corn 65
cot 32
cotton 65
cousin 40
cover 94
cow 4
cowboy 40
crab 4
crane 72
crawl 94
crayon 81
cream 55
cress 55
crew 41
crisps 55
crockery 32
crocodile 5
crocus 65
crow 5
crowd 41
cry 94
cub 5
cucumber 55
cup 32
cupboard 32
currants 56
curry 56
curtains 32
cushion 32
custard 56
customer 41
cut 94
cutlery 32
cycle 94

Dd
dachshund 5
dad 41
daddy longlegs 5
daffodil 65
daisy 65
Dalmation 5
dam 81
damson 56
dance 94
dandelion 65
dark 81
date 56
daughter 41
day 101
December 100
decorator 41
deer 5
dentist 41
desert 21
dessert 56
detective 41
diamond 81
diary 81
dig 94
dinghy 72
dining room 32
dinner 56

dinosaur 5	factory 21	garlic 66	headteacher 43	jockey 43
dirty 81	fair 22	gas 83	heather 66	jodhpurs 51
disc jockey 41	fall 95	gate 33	hedge 66	joiner 43
disco 81	family 42	gather 95	hedgehog 8	judge 44
dish 32	farm 22	gerbil 7	heel 50	jug 33
dive 94	farmer 42	giant 42	helicopter 73	juggernaut 73
diver 41	fawn 6	gipsy 42	helmet 84	juggler 44
dock 21	feathers 82	giraffe 7	help 95	juice 57
doctor 41	February 100	girl 43	hen 8	July 100
dog 5	feed 95	give 95	herbs 66	jump 95
doll 81	feet 50	glass 83	hero 43	jumper 51
dolphin 5	felt tip 82	glasses 83	heroine 43	junction 24
donkey 6	fence 33	glider 73	heron 8	June 100
door 32	fern 65	gloves 51	herring 8	jungle 24
doughnut 56	ferry 72	glue 83	hide 95	junk 73
dove 6	field 22	goat 7	hill 23	
down 93	fifth 99	gold 83, 98	hippopotamus 8	**Kk**
dragonfly 6	fifty 99	goldfish 7	hit 95	kangaroo 9
drain 32	fig 56	gondola 73	hoe 84	kayak 73
draw 95	fight 95	goose 7	hold 95	kennel 24
drawer 33	fill 95	gooseberries 57	holly 66	kettle 34
dress 51, 95	film 82	gorilla 7	honeysuckle 66	kick 95
dressing gown 51	fingers 50	gorse 66	hop 95	kilt 51
dressing table 33	fir 65	grandchild 43	horse 9	king 44
drifter 72	fire 82	grandfather 43	hose 85	kingfisher 9
drill 81	fire engine 72	grandmother 43	hospital 23	kiss 95
drink 95	fireman 42	grapes 57	hot 85	kitchen 34
drive 95	fire station 22	grass 66	hotdog 57	kite 85
driver 41	fireworks 82	grasshopper 7	hotel 23	kitten 9
drizzle 81	first 99	gravy 57	hour 101	kiwi 9
drop 95	fish 6	green 98	house 23	knee 50
drought 81	fish cake 56	greenhouse 22, 83	hovercraft 73	knife 34
dry 82	fisherman 42	grey 98	hundred 99	knit 95
duck 6	fish finger 56	greyhound 8	husband 43	knock 96
duffel coat 51	five 99	grocer 43	husky 9	koala 9
dustbin 33	flag 82	guinea pig 8	hut 23	
dustbinman 42	flamingo 6	guitar 83	hutch 23	**Ll**
	flats 22	gun 84	hyacinth 66	laboratory 24
Ee	fleece 83	gymnasium 22	hydrofoil 73	Labrador 9
eagle 6	florist 42			laburnum 67
ear 50	flour 57		**Ii**	ladder 85
earrings 82	flower 65	**Hh**	ice 85	lady 44
earthquake 82	fly 7, 95	hail 84	iceberg 85	ladybird 9
ear wig 6	foal 7	hair 50	ice cream 57	lake 24
east 82	fog 83	hair dresser 43	ice skates 85	lamb 10, 58
Easter egg 56	football 83	hair drier 84	icing 57	lamp 34
eat 95	football boots 51	hall 23, 33	igloo 23	lane 24
editor 42	forest 22, 65	ham 57	in 93	larch 67
eel 6	fork 33	hamburger 57	infant 43	laugh 96
egg 56	forty 99	hammer 84	inn 23	launch 73
eight 99	four 99	hamster 8	insect 9	launching pad 24
eighth 99	fourth 99	hand 50	inside 93	launderette 24
eighty 99	fox 7	handbag 84	into 93	lavender 67
elbow 50	freezer 33	handkerchief 84	iron 33, 95	lawn 24
electrician 42	freighter 72	hanger 23	island 24	leaf 67
elephant 6	Friday 100	hang glider 73	ivy 67	leek 58
elm 65	fridge 33	happy 84		legs 50
emu 6	friend 42	harbour 23	**Jj**	lemon 58
encyclopedia 82	frog 7	hare 8	jacket 51	lemonade 58
engine 72	funny 83	harp 84	jaguar 9	leopard 10
engineer 42		hat 51	jam 57	leotard 51
envelope 82	**Gg**	hawk 8	January 100	letter box 34
escalator 72	gale 83	hawthorn 66	jeans 51	lettuce 58
eyes 50	galleon 72	hay 66	jeep 73	librarian 44
	garage 22, 33	head 50	jelly 57	library 25
Ff	garden 22, 33	headphones 84	jet plane 73	lie 96
face 50			jig saw 85	

lifeboat 74
lift 74, 96
lighthouse 25
lightning 85
lightship 74
lilac 67
liner 74
lion 10
lips 50
little 85
lizard 10
lobster 10
lollipop 58
long 85
lorry 74
lounge 34
lumberjack 44
lupin 67

Mm
mackerel 10
magician 44
magpie 10
mail van 74
maize 67
make 96
mammal 10
mammoth 10
manager 44
map 85
March 100
margarine 58
marigold 67
market 25
marmalade 58
marsh 25
mason 44
mat 34
matches 86
mattress 34
May 100
mayor 44
measles 86
meat 58
mechanic 44
medicine 86
meet 96
melon 58
mend 96
microphone 86
milk 58
mill 25
mince 58
mincemeat 59
miner 44
minibus 74
mint 67
minute 101
mirror 34
mistletoe 67
mittens 51
mix 96
moat 25
moccasins 51
module 74
mole 10

monastery 25
Monday 100
money 86
monk 45
monkey 10
monorail 74
month 101
moon 25, 86
moor 25
moped 74
morning 101
mosquito 11
motel 25
moth 11
mother 45
motorboat 74
motorcycle 75
motorway 25
mountain 25
mouse 11
mouth 50
mow 96
mower 86
mumps 86
museum 26
mushroom 59, 67
musician 45
mutton 59

Nn
nails 50, 86
narcissus 68
narrowboat 75
near 93
neck 50
needles 86
neighbour 45
nephew 45
nest 11
nettle 68
new 86
newsagent 45
newsreader 45
newt 11
niece 45
night 101
nightdress 51
nine 99
ninety 99
ninth 99
nose 50
November 100
nun 45
nurse 45
nursery 26
nuts 59

Oo
oak 68
oars 86
oasis 26
oats 59
observatory 26
ocean 26
October 100
octopus 11

off 93
office 26
oilrig 26
old 87
omelette 59
on 93
one 99
onion 59
open 96
optician 45
orange 59, 98
orangutan 11
orchard 26
orchestra 87
organ 87
orphan 46
osprey 11
ostrich 11
otter 11
outback 26
outside 93
over 93
overalls 51
owl 12
ox 12
oyster 12

Pp
paddle 87
paint 87, 96
palace 27
palm 68
pan 34
pancake 59
panda 12
panda car 75
pansy 68
panther 12
pants 51
paper 87
parachute 75
park 27
parrot 12
party 87
passenger 46
pastry 59
pat 96
patient 46
pavement 27
peach 59
peacock 12
pear 59
peas 60
pebbles 87
pelican 12
pencil 87
penguin 12
perch 13
petal 68
petrol 87
pheasant 13
photograph 87
pianist 46
piano 88
pick 96
picnic 60

pie 60
pier 27
pig 13
pigeon 13
pike 13
pilot 46
pine 68
pineapple 60
pink 98
pizza 60
plaice 13
plant 68, 96
plate 34
play 96
playground 27
plimsoles 52
plug 34
plum 60
plumber 46
polar bear 13
police officer 46
police station 27
pond 27
pony 13
poppy 68
porch 34
pork 60
porridge 60
porter 46
post box 88
postman 46
post office 27
potato 60
pour 96
pram 75
prawn 13
priest 46
primrose 68
prince 46
princess 46
print 96
printer 47
pudding 60
puffin 13
pull 96
pullover 52
pupil 47
puppet 88
puppy 13
purple 98
purse 88
push 96
pyjamas 52
python 14

Qq
quay 27
queen 47
queue 47
quilt 35

Rr
rabbi 47
rabbit 14
racket 88
radiator 35

radio 88
radish 60
raft 75
railway 75
rain 88
rainbow 88
raincoat 52
raisin 60
rake 96
ranch 27
ranger 47
rapids 27
raspberries 61
rat 14
rattlesnake 14
read 96
recorder 88
record player 88
red 98
reed 68
referee 47
reindeer 14
reporter 47
reptile 14
reservoir 27
restaurant 28
rhinoceros 14
rhubarb 61
rice 61
ride 96
ring 88
river 28
robin 14
rocket 75
roll 96
roller skates 88
roof 35
rook 14
roots 69
rope 89
rose 69
round-about 28
rounders 89
rowing boat 75
rubber 89
rug 35
ruler 89
run 97
runway 28

Ss
saddle 89
safari park 28
sailor 47
salad 61
salmon 14
salt 61
sand 89
sandals 52
sandwich 61
sardine 14
Saturday 100
sauce 61
sausage 61
saw 89, 97
scales 89